MW01181167

GLENNA LUSCHEI

· ·

NEW AND SELECTED POEMS

Libido Dreams

For Amy:
a poet after
my own heart.
Warm wishes.
gratitude for
the Prairie

Glenna
Sept 18, 20 17

ARTAMOPRESS

SANTA BARBARA · CALIFORNIA

Published by
ARTAMO PRESS

Artamo Press, first edition, 2007
Copyright © 2007 by Glenna Lusschei

Permissions acknowledgements appear on page 5.

Artamo Press is a division of Artamo LLC.

Book and cover design by Jack N. Mohr

Library of Congress Control Number: 2007928071
ISBN 978-0-9788475-4-8

www.artamopress.com

Printed on acid-free paper in the United States of America

ACKNOWLEDGMENTS

The author gratefully acknowledges the following publications where several of the poems in this volume first appeared:

"Our Four Corners," "Feeding Fish by Flashlight," "Bare Root," "Birches," "Imposter," "Snapped," and "I Thought They Would Never End" in *Seedpods* (PRESAPRESS, 2006); "Our Four Corners" and "Gang Wars and Galapagos" reprinted in *ASKEW* (2006); "Passing through Sleep" and "Snapped" reprinted in *The Sorrow Psalms* (UNIVERSITY OF IOWA PRESS, 2006); "Time Is the Canoe" in *Blue Ark West* (2006); "Gang Wars and Galapagos" in *Cairn* (2006); "Champagne Toast," "I'm Listening," and "Treading on Plums" in *Pembroke* (2005, 2007); "I'd Trade My Horse and Dog" in *South Dakota Review* (2000); "The Portuguese Explorer That I Am" and "The Vietnamese Princess" in *Art Life* (2003, 2005); "Unnamed" in *Chance of a Ghost* (HELICON EDITIONS, 2005); "Kestrel" in *Parnassus* (2005); "Occupation," "Single," "The Feldspar Mine," "Petroleum," "El Cenote" "Cricket Box," and "Passing through Sleep" in *Shot With Eros* (JOHN DANIELS & COMPANY, 2002), "Reservoir," "Pianos around the Cape," and "Inland Passages" in *Pianos Around the Cape* (ASPERMONT PRESS, 1999); "Throwing away My Shoes in Tokyo" in *Unexpected Grace* (TURKEY PRESS, 1984).

CONTENTS

CONTENTS

IN SILENCE

CONTENTS

If a separate personal Paradise exists for each of us,
I reckon mine must be irreparably planted with trees
of words the wind silvers like poplars, by people who
see their confiscated justice given back, and by birds
that even in the midst of the truth of death insist on
singing in Greek and saying, 'eros, eros, eros.'

— Odysseas Elytis

For Hugh

FOUR CORNERS
OF LOVE

OUR FOUR CORNERS

Whenever there is water someone is drowning.
— Robert Bly

Friends, consider that we have always lived
under the narcosis of water lilies.
This room is the aquarium and we are all dreaming
within it. Remember how our teachers held us
until the sun lit up seaweed in late afternoon?
Afterwards in the castle, bride and groom.
We never questioned our four corners.

When the Buddhist master married us
he said, "You cannot love anyone in this life
you have not loved in your first body
of water." That is why we come in different shapes
and sizes. There is room in the ocean
for the doll, the skull and the anchor.
When you find someone she has always
been there. When you lose someone
he is treading the water near you.

SINGLE

You always loved the red madrone.
It may well have been the only one
in San Luis Obispo County.
We hiked there through private
property.

At night while my children slept,
you went out
to pee with my collie. At dawn leapt
the fence. When their father took them
for Xmas, you invited me home to Oregon.

Your mother,
only a little younger than me, knitted
warm slippers for my cold feet.
She told me how you children loved to watch
rain spill over the fire wood.

I loaned you the station wagon
to interview in the Valley.
After you moved I pulled on boots to visit
the red madrone.
Rain tore off its bark in the sheets.

KESTREL

Dammit! I couldn't send you a Val-
entine this year; I drove you... I mean
your ashes to Yosemite.

When I saw you in your mask
I swerved into the fence post
but you perched again and

again, kestrel beside crow on the high
tension wire, everywhere along the Grapevine.
In the Lodge, too, the Kachina figure

of the kestrel said endurance.
The turtle on your garment said energy
from underground. In your codicil

you requested Delphi, the navel of the world.
Sure, I would chew those laurel
leaves for you, shimmy down the crevice

and screech my prophecy, "You'll fry in Hell
for leaving me!" Fat lot of good that would do.
So I hike... unsteady on the ice to

Bridal Veil Falls, throw a fist full of you
into the mist. My nostrils catch grit
flying back. Not bad.

Kestrel's message from underground:
Endurance. I couldn't get rid
of you if I tried.

Be Mine.

I'M LISTENING

Dutchman's breeches: sky will clear.

Tick   tick   the old Dutch clock kept me
awake   I stayed   it snowed in goose
down. Rain pouring
one patch of blue.

Tick tick, out the door.   Taxi
in the snow. Driver from Ghana his wife
was a drummer.   I'm listening
through drum
          smoke
                    the clock.

I told you everything. When you lost hearing
aids we sifted through vacuum bags, swept
clippings at the barber shop. Not the furnace?
We found them in your mahogany
bed stand. How can I find you?

New Year's Eve
fumes of retsina smashed
the hearth. I nearly lifted
my glass. I swear
I heard you say, "Kali." Speak
to me though smoke.

This year I promise: your ashes to Delphi.
Speak to me through the Oracle.
I know they deserve better than the plastic
bag next to my biking helmet. Say something
anything to me now.

You Can't Turn it Back

Once you start something moving
you can't turn it back.

That painful afternoon
I persuaded my kindergarten
teacher to march the class to the chick
pea garden. In the morning
it sparkled yellow, blue, lilac and pink.
When we got there, all the blossoms
had withered under heat.

No one would believe me again.

Decades later, I learned the word
ephemeral. Grab it when you can.
and the word *inexorable.* Once set
in motion it won't turn back.
The Model T wasn't going too fast.
Tippy wasn't chasing it
but he got caught

under the wheels. He high tailed
it back to the yard and died
in my arms. I couldn't do anything
but watch it all play out.

That bright morning when my children
and ex drove off for Alaska, the man
who broke up my marriage and I

strolled through a field of chick peas.
All of a sudden he vanished.

Scared, I discovered him
hiding face down in the vines.

What a jerk. But what has been started
must be played out.

CRICKET BOX

When you opened the door
I stood back
to absorb the aroma of sandalwood
the full glow of the Tiffany lamp
over the grand piano
the Fortuny-upholstered chair

and then invited in,
I entered

to give you the thing I brought from China.
A thousand years ago the emperor's son
opened the cricket box
to insert the hinged
creature.
I thought my gift exotic, now obscene
as the connoisseurs who shackled apes
beneath the table to taste the
brain, alive and warm.

The potter drilled
those perfect breathing vents
into clay but I
brought this gift for you.
I thought you would take me out
into your dazzling sandblasted
city, introduce me to friends. Even
show my poems around.

You said, "I want to keep you
to myself."

You offered me the finest:
Stolichnaya, Sevruga Caviar.
Once you said, "Would you like
sex?" You opened the Encyclopedia
Britannica, eleventh edition,
and showed me how the parts
fit together.

OCCUPATION

The moon was done up
in knitting needles
in the land where you loved.

You changed your name
when you went to bars. You said
the girls
loved you for your kind
eyes. They were starving.

You said she knew
her place.   I didn't
measure up.
Not sexy
enough,
not implacable
enough.

She became my occupation.
I saw her bound up in pink obi.

I went to Japan for myself.
Women surrendered
to me, too.
The old woman scrubbed my back
in the o-furo.

You brought back a fan from Japan
for the girl you would marry.
It smelled of sandalwood
when I snapped it.

Rain Dance

Twenty years of waiting for him
to apologize, to ask me to dance.
I asked him

and we danced at our son's wedding
to his Mexican beauty. Two hours
with Mariachis, all night with DJs.
Salsa, meringue, samba, cha-cha-cha.
Even to *Smoke Gets in Your Eyes,*
while the machine threw out smoke.

And on the bronzed California hills,
it began to rain as in the green
corn dance at Zia Pueblo. It rained down
mudhens, kashares, crickets, lightning
bugs and lightning. The Wall
broke into wet crumbling adobe.
Our grandchildren slid down the berm
like salamanders.

And I forgave him,
understood why smoke
got in my eyes, why lovely things die,
why I loved him.
The shine on our children's faces
when they saw us dancing
made me grieve for our estrangement.
Our children, with splits in their heads
like Frankenstein's monster, would not heal,

become whole, until I merged with the other
half of the nucleus. I grieved
that I withheld this peace from them.

And we danced in the rain until dawn
until all the roses fell upon our path.

ECLIPSE

While the husband worked
she grew into her redwood house
as in her childhood story
of people who merged with oak
trees.

When she was thirty she awoke to acorns
dropping on her roof.
She knew she would be initiated
into the rite of trees
during the lunar eclipse.

She crept out and spied the tangled
red yarn in the moon.
Blood lines in the moon.
She ventured one foot into the tree bark.
It yielded and she entered the tree.

She slept there until she heard
her husband chopping wood.

She gave him a basket of red
yarn. He grew plump and one day said,
"This house no longer suits me."

When they moved on
her necklace caught on the pump handle.
Pearls scattered
under the redwood deck.

She wondered if the wagon would bring
her back one day; if pearls
would have grown into mushrooms.

JEALOUSY

Jealousy crouches
beneath the breast
bone, steals the breath,
awakens the night.

Is that what ate the fish?
Only yesterday a scummy,
sunny, fertile lotus pond.
All we believed in:
beauty arises from filth
breaks through clouded waters.

Without the fish and the papyrus
jealousy abandons its kill.
All that remains is clear, cool, sterile...

ADOBE

I learn
the bricks are covered
with chicken wire
then plastered.

We become friends
instead of lovers.

You remain the stranger
with the long, narrow back

cutting sand into cement.

THE FELDSPAR MINE

When we were married
my husband said to me,
"You're a natural resource
I want to share the wealth."
He gave me second best —
I squandered myself.

He saw me as the feldspar mine
with mica spilling out.
"O golden one
tumble down the grade.
Be free, *mi dorada*
illuminate
the pegmatite and quartz."

But when I'm in my grave
will they remember how I shone?
At night when the red tides
flash
will they say
"That's the sea nymph back
for one last splash?"

Oh, why don't I preserve my gold
in one lead casket?
Do I still have time
to comb the mine
for banded agates?
I'm not fished out!

The sea comes up in a breaststroke,
a marathon swimmer the sea:
"You've half a lifetime left,
Go home, home!"

El Cenote

Throughout the fifty-two year
Mayan calendar,
they never
understood their love,
bottomless as the cenote,
the jaguar
with his jade eye.

Her lament: loss, loss.
He complained
she burned the rice,
spilled the masa,
wept.

In that lake
she would recover
all she had lost.
If he let her go
for that new water sprite
she would dive
through the castles
and parapets
to discover
skeletons of lost love.

She could not hear
him purr, the jaguar
on the altar
of El Castillo.

She stitched loss
into her wimple.

They could not
accept
the bottomless
lake
they were offered.
They were not
Abelard and Heloise,
they were mortal.

THE SILVER CROSS

Alone. I rode the high
mesa. Winds forced me out
to graze with pinoñes.

Tony. Single, from Truchas
wore the silver cross of penitentes.
We hunted pine nuts, replaced
them with corn for squirrels.

His place: one room adobe,
bathroom, filthy.
Books lined four walls.

We made love. I went home to fry
tortillas. For Xmas he gave me
turquoise. I gave him the ouija board.
We never got good as J.M. and D.J.
but the oracle always said

yes.

Before I moved I gave him
blue hyacinth bulbs. Remember
me in spring!

Many springs, mine in trout stream,
his in snow, both hyacinth.

HERE

Love's in the daily doings
the blister on the first roasting chili
the race to gather sheets
at the wick of lightning.

We fold the linen with lavender
and sage.

Love's the oar that draws us to the sea.

You propel me over quick
silver waves to San Luis Obispo,
through spidery hills of black oak,
call me home.

The mica I bring you
scatters in my pocket,
but the Hunter Moon
tracks it to the tarmac.

Why scan the moon's two continents for love?

Our friends shout, "Look around!"

It's here beside us
on the dark side.

We fold the linen with lavender
and sage.

PASSING THROUGH SLEEP

Your voices splash
the mountain of my death

Lover   daughter

Your questions arch
like fish

The Egyptian priest
balances voices

Yours are equal
in sweetness and timbre

You will travel together

I the canyon
sounding echo

Lover   daughter

Leave your dialogue
(volcano and ash)

I cross over
the bridge of a phrase

in no hurry

going to visit Ixtaccihuatl
loved for aeons.

Petroleum

It took me years to find the peony
but it all came back
with its wild blooms —
scalded chicken feathers.

When I smelled the peony I remembered
the millennia, lives I was meant
for, all laid out.
You were there.
We were the same body, separated
by the big bang, jetted into the system,
doomed to reunite.

I buried that love deeply. Only years
could excavate the gingko tree
that lived with dinosaurs. Only the years
could retrieve the peony whose DNA
ants lug up and down the stem,
the peony who outlives its planters
as we outlive our parents.

It's all there, the ginkgo tree that loves
pollution, its memory of petroleum
and my liquid palm
meant to grasp your stem.

SNAPPED

Acorns so thick we skated through them!
We cracked the buckeye
and the chestnut cask
beneath our boots.
The wooly worm, orange
turned black, augured
for the one-hundred-year's frost.
Farmers predicted ice.

Telephone poles snapped.
No power in the Blue Ridge.
We opened our house,
laid a fire with hickory.
We served black-eyed peas
and grits to kin.
Blizzard turned to sacrament.

That other New Year's
you and I scaled Blowing Rock.
The Cherokee maiden implored
the winds to blow her fallen lover
back from the cliff.

I pressed to drag you back
from the winds that tore you,
until something
in me snapped.
I had to let the snow enfold you.

BIRCHES

Love belongs to the North
— Tom McGrath

I crave the snow,
dream it everywhere
crusted on rows and rows
of poles on barges
as we encompass the Artic Circle.

No they're birches with white bark
not snow at all.

My children carved their first
letters to me on birch bark:

I love you, love you...

BACK INTO MY BODY

My mother is dying.

I give her a bath — she's pregnant
with death
swollen belly and one nipple gone
where I bit down as a baby.

I'm taking her back into my body.

My mother is pulling silk
from the cocoon
not to lose the thread.
She's larva again.

She's taken her hands
from my shoulders
no longer yells
"Straighten up!"
Death has come to take her back
and only the well
pass blame.

Worms are at work in her veins.

Only the beautiful
hide their breasts and you
naked as a spool
have arranged the linens
for one last time
and touched the cranberry glass.

In the fight for your antiques
leave me nothing.
I'm alive
and strong with you back in my spine.
I lift you from your bath

and dry
and love you.

COUNTRY

The first time I walked with Bill
he put peppermint from the café

into my palm and closed my hand
around it.

In San Francisco he chased
my straw hat under the trolley.

I knew he would take care of me.
We loved Paris but we were country.

Like Collette I serve our friends
coq au vin from unmatched casseroles.

We skipped back a generation
to become my grandparents.

We walk to the post office
by day, track snails for supper.

Champagne Toast: Travels through War and Life

CHAMPAGNE TOAST
— for Hugh

We knew elegance
was holding champagne
but we favored red wine,
the color of our dancing shoes.

We turned afternoons
and evenings into glamour,
noses to the host.
Strange that we look so alike.

Secrets underlie the instant
of light on water,
the water striders on pontoons.

We seize our glasses
toasting on the edge of what
rises and drifts down river.

The tongue dissolves.

All we need is a breeze
to lift us to our bed
overlooking the forest.
We perished for the city,
the crowd we thought we knew.

Sleeping In

We had night
work to do, weaving with spiders
hammering back barrel staves.

The family that raised me dozed
long after the collie brought up the paper
after the mailman's retreat.

We worked through tribal
memory: buffalo driven off the cliff
in the Black Hills. Children like us
bundled into bloody carcasses
for warmth.

With the muted voice of owls
memory spit up pelt.

Women riding to homesteads
in covered wagons
stitched their own shrouds
with their babes' layettes. Today
women with children walk
hours at night to escape amputation.

Children like us
in orphanages
until they run out of wood
learn to hammer
coffins for each other.

BLACKBERRY WINTER

After the first heat
of spring
weather turned cold,
white blackberry
blossoms: Memorial
Road.

Old infected maples,
one for each soldier
except African
Americans, cut down.
New trees, one
for everyone, reach out,
"Come to me."

In the cemetery
of the old home place,
no markers for the slaves.
They still cry out,
"Come to me."

The Wooden House

Four generations live here,
each given a task.

Spinning the wool goes to Marina
with plenty of spit to guide the thread,
a bowl of cranberries at her elbow.

Embroidery is next.
Anna will dream of the one she loves
sleeping on the stitched pillow.

The healer to lather you with birch
down to toes and fingers.
The astringent scent leaves
your body floating.

There must be room for a poet here.
even with the ill-tempered Banick,
God of the sauna. It's the only place
fortunes are told, where
the soul is cured.

LIBIDO DREAMS

The search light copter
vibrated my house,

hunting for the Siberian
tiger in my dream. Escaped
from the Moscow
circus, he snapped at a whip,
pulled against the lead
in my left hand.

My right hand guided
a three-eyed dog.
Right side warped
left side healthy and roaring.

Search light
since the last dream:

I met an anaconda in the forest
who tried to lure me back but
I promised to attend the gala.

At dinner I shrieked
at the anaconda settled in my lap,
coiling up to the red wine.

Amber

Try as you might
you can't escape the vessel.
Here we are
popped out in Copenhagen
where men wear top hats.
Skyscrapers carry domes, too.

At the Danish-Modern Lutheran
Church, two Mormon missionaries
befriend us.
They usher us down the line-up
of severe apostles.
Peter holds the keys to the kingdom.

Everyone's on a mission.
The Buddhist tourist scurries
to capture the Little Mermaid.
Marble on rock, she sits forever
back to the sea.

I chase my own passion:
Amber! Resin locked in trees
for 53 million years. A mosquito's
pinned down, wings back.
Not a bad way to spend eternity.

I'd Trade My Horse and Dog

I'd trade my horse and dog
for my Lakota Sioux,
who put on my chapeau
and danced a poem around the prison room
for us.

He started a journal, at last wrote a poem
about his beautiful mother
who died when he was born.

He went on to know a dozen mothers.
His shaman father taught him the healing
dances, the eagle rite-of-passage for braves;
but he became berdache,
took the female spirit role.
If only he could bring back his mother!

No Hiawatha this Sioux
but his great eyes lit our prison room.
I was born in Sioux City, too.

Every week I wore a more outrageous hat.
Ribbons, birds, a wigwam, the Floyd Monument.
Sioux would model them.
Her poems soared: the eagle feathers
we discovered in the yard.

In Sioux's vision the guards attacked me.
She blessed me with white sage
from the sweat lodge,
named me "dancing words away."

After Xmas she came to class less;
finally quit.
I called her quad —
I'd trade my horse & dog
to heal her wrist.

BILL OF LADING

My passport has arrived.
It's time to move on.
I own my books and the dining room table.
My mother shipped it from Iowa
when they ran the highway
through our house.

Here I ladle Brunswick stew
I learned in North Carolina.
I publish books from this table,
elect the president.

One guest,
Camilo Torres, priest,
brought Marxist students to my house
the night before I left Bogotá.
Possessions stacked in cartons,
I listened for Colombian revolutions.
Waiters in black tie
served champagne.

One month later
I saw Camilo in *La Prensa*
dead
eyes still open.

I can't blame my table for what happened
in the Andes
for the highway through the plains.

Poets write.
Revolutions form.
Hear a baby cry every morning.

INJECTION

In Bogotá where children slept on streets
under bullfight posters
three figures reach out of the dark.

The woman wears herringbone. She touches
my arm. "Señora,
Señora, this is my daughter, and her baby
is sick. Could you give us money?"

I am in my twenties.

I reason —
if I give her pesos
she may buy *aguardiente.*

I take her to the pharmacy
stark with light.
Its smells of ether.
The druggist gives the baby an injection.

Years later, I wonder why I didn't ask their story.
Why were they in the street at dusk?

I had to buy meat for my family. I hurried
home to supper.

Throwing Away My Shoes in Tokyo

How can I toss these shoes
into the trash?
They carried me to every shrine in Kyoto.

They stood outside inns and bathhouses
faithful as the dog at Shibuya Station
forever awaiting his master.

They protected me on bullet trains
got muddied while the doctor
wearing rubber boots
showed me where to pick strawberries.

I might have left them at the Shogun's Palace
where the cricket boards chirp
when an intruder approaches the bedchamber.
These shoes sounded warnings.

They were black patent leather,
dressy to the last.

FLYING INTO THE FIRE

You're a veteran of four wars.
In Vietnam you turned to
your dead co-pilot
and saw the fear still on his face.

When you went home with the body
his mother asked,
"Why wasn't it you instead?"

In Jerusalem a bomb
killed your wife
while she sat with you on the park bench.

Now I fly into the fire.
I have escaped death
too many times,
I won't rest until all the children
have enough to eat.

Unnamed

My name is only known
to the pear tree
on Lexington

the forsythia
whipping the Park,
the starlings
that sing me awake
while the shark moon
bottoms out
with the lamps.

My name will be known
in the potter's field
where unnamed children
are carried down the ramp.
Prisoners bury them
50 cents an hour.

The sign above the cemetery
at Hart Island
reads:
Don't cry for us.
We are at peace.

VETERANS

We take off our shoes. Japanese style.
I'm glad I changed my socks.

Tsunami-san, your name
like the tidal
wave, crashes over me.
In Hokkaido I slept in your six-tatami room
head on a rice pillow.

You taught me to cook shabu-shabu:
enhoki mushrooms, chrysanthemum leaves
in broth. Confused, I called it Basho-Basho.

Knowing I loved poets and books,
you took me to see paper-making.
I expected kozo drying.
Logs floated in one end,
bales of newsprint tumbled out the other.

When I married, you visited my home.
You and my husband, young sailors,
fought at Midway. Opposite sides.

At night we went to the funeral
of the Marine Colonel we knew.
Someone said, "Those veterans are going out
fast."

Tsunami-san, I was impatient at the time.
But thank you for making me go through
the whole factory. Thank you for signing
my guestbook in kanji. That tanka
about the plum tree that bloomed
even when the master was far away.

I Thought They Would Never End

I thought they would never end
the walks through the meadow of the blue vervain
where the heron nested in eucalyptus.

I thought they would always remain
my four blue eggs.

I thought my luck would never end.
I would hoist up one skein of flounder after another.
Loaves would fall into my open hands.
Look.   Oh look.

I think my life will never end.
How lazily I go about it.
Every day will open morning glories.

Can my world stay the same
no boundary wars   no bombings?
I put my teapot on and lose my head again in steam.

PIANOS AROUND THE CAPE

At last we found Happy Valley
and the long walkway to the house
my husband's great-great-grandfather
saved from burning in the Civil War.

In amber light,
we traced his family back through twenty
layers of wallpaper adjoining fireplaces
in every room.
During Stoneman's Raid
the slaved hid in chambers behind the hearth.
We laid hands on the worn-down bricks
they used for carving stones.

After the War, the brothers, California bound
shipped their pianos around the Cape.
The sisters and the mothers filed to the Pacific
Ocean to do their wash.
They dried long skirts on cypress branches.
Cattle ate the cloth for salt.

IMPOSTER

In the dream, under the dying moon,
I am scrubbing the sidewalk.
In the dark, I shed my robe:
Ishtar, entering a new life.

The next act: a theatre.
I am outfitted
for the underworld:
a black suit, a matinee hat.

When I descend to the Orpheum
the exit lights flash. Go!

People offer me free
tickets but I am afraid authorities
will blow the whistle.

THE VIETNAMESE PRINCESS

One foggy beach night
winding my way back from the prison
through the eucalyptus grove
she flickered in my headlight.
That young woman in odai racing
her motorcycle across the sand
didn't make a sound.
The tails of her garment and black hair
flew behind her as she receded
into fog. This ghost was chasing someone.

In his yarns of the Vietnamese netherworld,
Vi enchanted our class with her doomed life.
When someone had too much rice
it was her destiny to even it out, take a life.
She lived where children sobbed
for their mothers, where mothers
searched for their babes. Once a princess,
she even frightened royalty.

When the fog rolled in, Vi's stories unnerved
me. I requested an officer
to escort me to my pickup.
Vi was a gentle soul. Hard to believe
he murdered his wife. His English
wasn't perfect but I'm sorry I gave him a B.

They Let Us Shoot, Too

As our ship docks at St. Petersburg
a brass band plays *Lara's Theme*
and *Dixie*.

The Russian soldier in black pumps
turns her back on the camera
but no one says, "Nyet, Nyet."

Everyone says, "Dollar, dollar"
for postcards, lacquer boxes and nesting dolls.

Today's special: stroganoff invented
for Prince Stroganoff's bad teeth.
Still delicious!

You forget you're in Russia
until you ask for a bathroom
and the guide asks, "Is it an emergency?"

The reconciliation of prince
and swan: an evil spell cast off.

Brides stand for photographs before the statue
of Peter the Great. They let us shoot, too.

I buy a babushka to keep the rain from stinging.
It's spring. You can't hold it back.

For the Space Shuttle Columbia

Better than 20/20.
The eyes of a jet pilot, my doctor tells me.

In my mind's eye, one
jet split from the squadron.

I want glasses to see into the gem of ocean,
to crack the treasure.

I want the instinct of the leaders of geese
to create that updraft that will keep our young ones.

When one is hurt, two geese fly down
till the one recovers or dies.

Give me the sight to know the hurt.
Let me see to the far-off Arctic nest
of the gooseneck barnacle.

Let me see beneath the earth where
we were intricately made,

fathom
our mysteries.

I pray for the periscope of the oxalis
straight up from underground. Let me see.

Let me bite the sour grass.

Gang Wars and Galapagos

When I said, *"Yo soy el interprete"*
the patient took my hand. Healing
happened there and then. I realized
language was the cure. "Your concern
is my concern. Your pain is my mission.
Don't be afraid. You will be heard."

Fidelina sat straight in her immaculate
cotton blouse, washed and ironed
a thousand times. I helped her
with her gown; we filled out the forms.
Growing up she worked in the *milpas*.
Her family could not afford the *cuadernos*
for writing the alphabet.
She never learned to read.

The gang stabbed Fidelina's son outside
the Seven-Eleven in Santa Maria.
The police never investigated. Now
she suffers from insomnia and depression.
The doctor took Fidelina's hand.
It's good for a psychiatrist
to watch the *interprete* break down and cry.

In the Galapagos, we walk up to the fuzzy
baby albatross, beak open, waiting for his next
meal. Since we aren't allowed to feed or touch
the birds don't live with fear.

Without predators the cormorant lost
his ability to fly. And I once believed
flight/fight was the only way to live.

THE PORTUGUESE EXPLORER THAT I AM
— for David

To find myself I became another.
   I who hate shopping purchased a boot
      strong enough to trek Tibet

and maps to point myself North.
   I ordered a trident, sphere, astolobe,
      and a dog for I could not bear to sail

without one on my ship. Oh yes, a ship,
   for navigating the Mekong Delta
      where Camões became landlocked.

The one I seek is also
   a Portuguese explorer and to reach him
      I must hack my way through cow-hoofed trees.

My destiny is in the hands of the Tarot reader
   one card away from trapped
      in the jungle, lost at sea.

IN SILENCE:
NATURE'S PASSAGE

In Silence

The deer glides down Manhattan's
arrowhead

In silence, in silence.

Invisible in snow, the deer trots,
leads me down
through our history,
when Powhattan sold Manhattan
and George Washington surrendered
his commission to his troops.

To the ancient marble customs house,
in silence to Ground Zero.

People in black weep by the fences.
Umbrellas over their heads
catch the snow.
The tarnished metal letters stand:
The World Trade Center PATH Station.

In silence, in silence.

The deer leads us through the snow.
I am invisible
but not afraid of the dark.

THE CARDINAL

North Carolina house sculpted in snow,
the cardinal, hot as a cinder
burns out his alphabet in the icy drive.

Yes!
carving new letters for January
I scrape my kabbala onto the windshield.

My dream?
They came to my house fasting
but the Brunswick stew:

country ham, black-eyed peas, onions,
corn, squirrel and a whole bottle of ketchup
gone.

Then the photograph in the magazine:
Sierra Leone's children with amputated arms.
No way to eat.

Sculpted in snow, alphabet in ice,
I carve letters with my breath.
Let me sing a new song.

For my new life, I must act fast.
I must fast, become the cardinal pecking frost.
My engine at last

catches hold. I drive to Lowe's
buy a feeder shaped like a bell
to remember the starved, the lost.

THE GREAT DISMAL SWAMP

Swamp for our meeting place
the Great Dismal
hidden between Carolina and tidewater

Virginia,   we were young then
up to cypress knees arched

　　　　black gum root.

When we heard Swainson's warbler
we slid down Jericho Ditch.

Run-away slaves found freedom:
couples eloped to marry.

No one returns from its heart
of 10,000 years watery growth
but we found our way home
from the forbidden

　　　　through forty.

TREADING ON PLUMS

The night of the Santa Anas,
wind swept blue plums off the trees.
They lie squashed on the berm:
terrapins with retracted heads
that clutter the highways of Arkansas.

The sweet-sour aroma of rotting plums
stirs up my parents
pouring choke-cherry nectar
through cheesecloth. They never said,
"Too busy." They stocked a cellar

full of jelly. My father who labored all day,
at night boiled rice for drifters
riding the rails through town. I listened
to their laments of losing farms,
licked jelly from the paraffin.

The night of the Santa Anas
I was too busy to gather blue plums
as wind swept them from the trees.

Feeding Fish by Flashlight

I leave them for the last of my chores
and by the time I finally shake out
their flakes they are no longer hungry,
rising to the top only out of politeness.

"Can't you come back tomorrow, but early?"
They would say. Is procrastination as bad
as pride, presuming we have all the time
in the world, and when we finally arrive

at midnight, knowing our nutrients flow
unheeded over the weir? Or seeing
our children near sleep, eyes half-hooded,
still waiting for their story?

Night Crawlers

The odor of rain on cement:
my Nebraska memories jolt
night crawlers from their dens.

My bare feet curled
scorching sidewalk.
Red ants crawled over my toes,
up my overalls.

When it stormed
I strode the puddles
not to trample the plush
night crawlers

a foot long,
pink tapering each end.
I would later learn their name
was Emperor

dissect their eight stomachs,
their two hearts.

I pushed the night crawlers
back into the grass
where they resumed their labor,
making life for us.

We were all workers in soil.
They manufactured the soft
earth that held up radishes.

Reservoir

I leap out on a watery day
and then walk on fog.
No different from walking on water.

By the time we get to the airport
it's clear
all the way to Sacramento.

We fly over a lake
new to me. The pilot calls out
San Luis Reservoir.

In Sacramento: peach
trees from my balcony. Blossoms
filter out the Capitol dome.
Later, trees
for each Civil War battle.
We listen for the soldiers.

I, too, come in and leave.
Light from the great windows
hollows out the Assembly.

Spirit sees my goings out
and comings in.

Legislation signed, we come home early.
The reservoir vanished
or else we took a different route.

No bumps.

At the airport I wait for my ride.
People come and go. Planes
land, take off.
At home I feed my dog.

Badger Pass Trail Head

Near Badger Pass Trail Head
a wounded animal hides.
Skiers lift over pocks of blood
chest forward as herons glide.
Deer test the lichen.
Coyote stalk the valley,
ears back.

On the surface there's something
for everyone
but Mirror Lake has turned to marsh.
Somewhere the animal limps
on ice.

He said, "Everything in nature
is resolved,"
but the trail of blood thickens.
She brings mystery to sugar pine,
skating on Ghost Forest Lake.
Snow enlightens her vision.

It's the equinox,
dark,
before she reaches shelter
at Ostrander Lake.
She rolls out her bag. She sleeps
alone.

HIEROGLYPHICS

My name with two N's
carries the Nile in it.

Let me be Water Bearer.
I may not pass this way again.

My name with an L
carries the lion.
With the papyrus frond
as E, I too make paper
and write upon it.

My name does not encase
the scarab though I love
the desert and the hot
Egyptian sun that climbs above it.

Remember the goddess
who in her blue robe
lies across the sky
connecting life and death.

I end with the A
the raven that cleans the carcass.

Beginning with G
my name starts with the jar.
Water Bearer let me be.
Lions go a long time
between kills.

BARE ROOT

These are unprotected sticks.
Not one leaf. I choose wisteria
to climb the oak,
life up hearty root stock
from the peat moss.

It's bare root season.
In this strange land
I yearn for the canopy
of foliage,
yearn for my old home.

Metamorphosis will come for me,
trans-movement through the light.
I will take hold, one day wear
the laurel. I dig, and learn
that I can tether; quick pain
is part of nature.

COPPERHEAD

Heat coils up.
The thermometer noses
to a hundred.

Gardening in the South-
look out! Don't give in to grief.

I know my hose
sidewinder.
Flickering sun.

Digging worms,
boys find the nest
of squirming copperheads.

They see me but never face
to face.
Tongue/the sun.

I remember eating
plaster
when I was pregnant.

A year later
I found a foot-long
roundworm in her diaper.

I dream my child back to life.
If I return to that South
I can find her.

THE TINDER BOX

You are far away.

States
are crossing blocks
I must step.
Rivers
dogs with copper eyes.

My starving mare
Eats
her mane.
The coals are watching us.

Bonfires.
Wigwams.

Inland Passages

Lakes in the Chugach Mountains
Flush out in a day.

In one night
The polluted metals of my life
Dissolve.
I must show my children
How to walk on mud.

Sun stays up
To forge me into gold
Though the moon furls out white
And grand as a Matanuska cabbage.

Juno, stirring up the moon,
Are you an alchemist?
Will you let me use your crystal
As crucible through trial?

Aren't you, too,
Cut apart from your mate?
You drift with me through inland passages
From Juneau
To Prince Rupert to Ketchikan
Down to the lower 48.

Time Is the Canoe

This morning I woke up
as a blue jay dove into wisteria.
I looked down when a loquat fruit
hit my foot.
Where did spring,
this industry come from?

Magnolias in water eradicate
musk from library stacks.

I cracked open a Brazilian
story, "The Third Bank." A man
hacks out a canoe and paddles the river
forever, through his daughter's wedding,
his son's rite of passage.
What is the meaning of the canoe?
His sarcophagus?

Time is the canoe.
We climb into our vehicles
leaving the ones who love us yearning.
We go unswerving. We do
what is to be done.